Simon Edwards

How to Start a
Podcast

A Complete Step by Step Guide
to Learn How to Create and Launch Your Profitable
Podcasting Business

Copyright © 2020 publishing.

All rights reserved.

Author: Simon Edwards

No part of this publication may be reproduced, distributed or transmitted in any form or by any means, including photocopying recording or other electronic or mechanical methods or by any information storage and retrieval system without the prior written permission of the publisher, except in the case of brief quotation embodies in critical reviews and certain other non-commercial uses permitted by copyright law.

Table of Contents

What is Podcasting? 6

So You Want To Be A Podcaster 13

What Makes Podcasting Different 17

Things to Consider Before Starting Your Podcast 22

Podcasting Software 25

How to Choose a Podcast Publishing Platform 28

Ten Simple Steps to Setting Up Your First Podcast 32

How to Choose a Topic For Your Podcast 38

Creating A Podcast 43

Can You Start A Podcast With No Money? 48

Can You Make Money Podcasting? 53

How To Create Your First Podcast 55

How to Make a Podcast Interactive 58

How to Make Your Podcast Newsworthy 61

Podcast Like A Pro 64

Ten Simple Steps to Setting Up Your First Podcast 74

How to Launch a Podcast 80

How To Use Podcasting To Build Your Business Online 83

Monetizing Your Podcast the Easy Way 88

5 Reasons to Transcribe Your Podcast 98

How To Use Podcasting To Build Your Business Online 100

How to Use Podcasting to Gain Authority For Your Business 105

The Trouble With Podcasting 113

What is Podcasting?

Do you have something interesting to share with people online? Are you an expert in some field curious about disseminating that knowledge regularly? Does one wish to possess more information about something but find the prospect of wading through many sites unappealing? Are you curious about details with a person's touch? If your answer to even one among the questions is yes, then Podcasting could also be the solution.

Podcasting stood for private On-Demand Broadcasting and was first used for iPods. There are several devices available within the market that will track podcasts.

Podcasting is the dissemination and downloading of audio and video data through the web. Podcasts started with people broadcasting their audio and shortly grew to accommodate other media and purposes, including rebroadcast of standard television and radio shows, classroom lecture sessions, public safety announcements, and election campaigning.

What makes Podcasting different from directly downloading audio and video files or streaming media files? The difference lies within the method by which the user learns about the supply of the data.

In case of regular downloads of media files, you'll encounter these files by following the links provided by an inquiry engine or an internet site hosting contents that interest you. A user can receive podcasts in three ways- by subscription, by syndication, or by automatic download. Podcatching client software collects distributed through RSS or Atom protocols whenever a replacement podcast posted. For the syndication of podcasts, the use of the client and contracts is essential.

Podcasts needn't accessed through these methods alone - frequently, podcasters make the podcasts available on their website for direct download. The podcast can thendownloaded to a computer or an mp3 player. On a computer, a daily media player is often wont to play the podcast. Alternatively, a VoIP service commonly used for podcasts.

An enhanced sort of Podcasting is out there during which images and time are synchronized. This will have educational uses to deliver slideshows, including audio from a lecture or for reading presentations from a foreign location.

Podcasting can help sick students or homeschoolers to urge the advantage of a daily classroom atmosphere through podcasts. Podcasting has immense potential in reaching students enrolled in distance education schemes too.

How Can They Help Your Business?

A podcast contrasts from a necessary download in that new substance might naturally conveyed. Clients need not click into your site for significant specials since the entirety of this data might be consequently downloaded. A podcast show comprises of a progression of individual scenes that you can tune in to and see on-line or disconnected at whatever point and any place you need.

While Podcasting has been around for around five years now strikingly, the term itself has just been around since 2004. It's a withdrawal of IPod (The most famous MP3 player) and broadcasting. Notwithstanding, you don't just have an MP3 player to tune in to programs. You can 'buy-in' to a whole podcast arrangement utilizing programming on your PC or tune in to a single scene at once by using an internet browser. Buying into podcast guarantees that every unique new show is consequently downloaded to your PC as they are distributed, and surprisingly better buying in is commonly free. The chance that you do happen to have an MP3 player, whenever you adjust your gadget, your podcasts will be downloaded for tuning in a hurry. If you would prefer not to buy in, but instead need a duplicate of a specific scene, you can tap the "Download" catch to spare to your hard circle. Once downloaded, you would then be able to oversee it and play it like you would some other sound record. What recognizes podcasts from different sound or video media is that the substance is open to its audience(s) at whatever point, any place, and anyway, they need.

What are the business applications of Podcasting? The podcast is an excellent favorable position for business explorers and salespeople who are continually in a hurry. Since they are often in travel, they can find out about what an organization is offering while they travel. They're ready to remain on the up and up to about changes that are happening in the business or a specific organization while in transit to their next gathering. At whatever point a business needs to change its advertising accentuation, their podcast will change with them. Podcasts empower potential clients to discover progressively about a specific organization and its scope of items and administration without feeling forced by a salesman. Or maybe, a benevolent voice is clarifying what improves the organization. One of a kind will serve to change over a potential customer into a client. Podcasts likewise save money on labor. A broad deal of power is ordinarily required to detail an organization's most up to date offers and advancements. With a podcast, guests click in and coordinated to any new data the organization needs to introduce. The other extremely extraordinary thing about podcasts is that they have an unimaginably broad reach. Customers from over the world can get to data on organizations or items and find out about them in a straightforward, direct way whenever, and without being attached to a PC.

Particularly significant is the usage of case cast registries, which rundown podcast appears alongside the connections to their unique sites. These catalogs expose accessible podcasts. Among the more famous of the podcast, records are Yahoo Podcasts, Odeo, Podcast Alley, and Podcasting News. When utilizing indexes, it's essential to choose sort and substance classifications that make it simpler for audience members to discover your podcast. When you recorded with a registry, you will start to get guests from these indexes to your site. To urge guests to listen to your podcast, you'll have to begin by making an alluring title that reveals to them only enough about your item to interest them. More significant than having an extraordinary claim, however, is having far superior substance.

A layout for your podcast will empower you to be sure you don't lose your audience, and spread all the focuses you need to hit. To what extent your podcast will be is legitimately identified with how a lot of news you need to share and the degree to which you can keep that news crisp and energizing. Recurrence of updates is likewise a significant issue to address. This will probably rely upon the idea of what you're talking about and how rapidly things change in that industry.

So You Want To Be A Podcaster

Do you think you have the stuff to contend in the detonating underground-industry of Podcasting and have an incredible idea for a Podcast?

Have you scratched the entirety of this off your rundown?:

o A Great Idea for a New Podcast!

o A Killer Script (No equivalent to an incredible idea)

o Recording Software

o A Microphone

o A Webpage (and a lot of data transmission)

o An RSS Feed for your Podcast scenes

o A Well Laid Out Plan on How to Market Your New Podcast

So how could you do it?

Is it true that you were ready to mark everything off the rundown? The vast majority of these things are important to make and host your podcast, and on the off chance that you haven't wasted time with a decent promoting arrangement yet? Keep your fingers crossed that your loved ones like the sound of your voice since it is improbable that numerous others will ever hear your Great New Podcast appear.

Try not to shoot the errand person. It is a cruel world out there with an excessive number of organizations seeking the equivalent Podcast crowd. What's that you state? Are we not discussing organizations? Just a free, gift-based, underground, podcast? That might be valid, yet the world of podcasting has become exponentially over the previous year, and that implies there are countless Podcasters out there who are viewing for a similar audience base that you are. Indeed, according to Forrester Research, by 2010, a large number of podcast shows ought to have around 12.3 million customary audience members.

Also, remember that the business world knows something to be thankful for when it sees it, bringing about more and more organizations getting on board with the Podcast fleeting trend in recent months.

However, that is alright; because there's still a lot of room in the Podcast Empire, and you can take in significant exercises from the business world.

They realize how to assemble a tasteful Podcast. They know how to advertise. They realize how to network. Furthermore, potentially most importantly, they realize how to showcase a Podcast. What's more, you can laugh at the corporations attacking the peaceful Podcasting Nirvana, all you need. However, the reality remains. If you need to get your new Podcast out to the majority, you would be advised to bone up on some Marketing Basics.

So, where do you start?

Indeed, one of the most important things that you can do is to comprehend and have working information on your business Value Chain. What's a Value Chain, you inquire? It is the legitimate progression of your new Podcast business, beginning with your original idea and finishing each progression until the completed item hits your audience's iPod.

Did you get that? As such, your Podcast's Value Chain comprises of the considerable number of steps you have to take to get your item under the control of your audience members.

A Podcast's Value Chain will comprise of 10 stages:

Idea - > Pre-creation - > Post-Production - > Publishing - > Hosting - > Promotion - > Community/Search - > Downloading - > Show Viewing

If you produce a podcast appear, you will address every one of these means. And keeping in mind that each progression may offer you a remarkable arrangement of difficulties, each will likewise furnish you with their opportunities to adapt and showcase your new show.

The Value Restraint of your Podcast Show will consistently be at the core of your endeavor, whether you use it or not. This being the situation, the more mindful you are of your Value Chain, the simpler it will become for you to exploit and benefit from each progression of the procedure.

What Makes Podcasting Different

At the point when the indications of new technology for creating web content showed up, no one knew about its development speed. Presently, after months, the Podcasting will be an ever-increasing number of well known and new distributors are creating content because of this technology. They have discovered this technique naturally and appealing to customers. Paying little mind to the entrancing parts of interactive media content, what different alternatives make the Podcasting not quite the same as different techniques for giving and distributing content? Here, I have recorded five significant contrasts. Maybe, at the time that you read this article, as this technology will be increasingly full-grown step by step, new reasons could be added to my rundown.

Despite other known techniques for conveying content, which is, for the most part, dependent on Push technology, the Podcasting depends on pull technology. In push technology, the substance is conveyed, guided from the source to the buyer. The purchaser does not influence it. For instance, when a radio channel begins at a particular time, follows dependent on a predefined and fixed program, and finishes at a particular time, the shopper gets no opportunity or authorization to modify any piece of it. On the off chance that you lose a piece of the program, you won't have the option to re-hear it out. You can not rewind it, stop it and ponder the subject then re-play it. This is push technology. In any case, that you could have control of the progression of the substance, it would be a pull. The customer chooses the substance and controls it. Podcasting is a sort of pull technology. You download the chosen substance, and use is dependent on your longing and full power over the progression of substance.

Anyway, there are many advising and programmed content syndication utilities. However, you ought to consistently surf various websites for various substances. This is your duty, as the purchaser of the substance, to proceed to visit the wellspring of the substance on a site. However, Podcasting evacuates this progression. Only one time, forever, you pick your longing radio channel, news source, writer channel, or the consequences will be severe. At that point, the accumulation programming would be mindful to convey the latest throws directly in your versatile MP3 player. Sooner or later, you would even overlook the location of websites, and simply tuning in to the downloaded cutting-edge substance would be your everyday design.

Web association isn't that much simple to be accessible without fail and all over the place. Thus, utilizing web substance would be inconceivable much of the time. At the point when you are driving, climbing, resting, and strolling in the first part of the day, you would be denied approaching web content. No weblog, no surfing, no radio channel, and else. Be that as it may, the downloaded podcasts are accessible in the MP3 player who could be available to you in various events and spots, preparing throws to utilize. No PC and telephone line to interface with the Internet is required. No spotless spot to sit and utilize your PC for surfing the sites is required. Everything stacked in your minor MP3 player, which can play hours with no compelling reason to power stopped.

The gadget for utilizing podcasts is a small, inevitably, and wherever accessible MP3 player. The iPod is a brand that is possessed by the Apple organization. It is the reason this technology is called Podcasting. The Pod is gotten from iPod and cast from Broadcast. The iPod isn't the main MP3 gadget that could utilize. There are various suppliers of MP3 player gadgets that the customer could use for tuning in to podcasts. These little gadgets are portable. Devour exceptionally low vitality to work. They are light and little. They are not costly and are accessible with various limits. MP3 players are well known, and you can see numerous individuals in the road that have balanced them over their neck and are tuning in to the music. They are presently part of the day by day life. It makes the entrance proportion of the podcasts further than another kind of substance that is essentially needy of having a PC, or PC and Internet association.

Plausibility of creating podcasts is high. It is modest and simple to create. From proficient radio channel proprietors to novice artists who have little audiences among their school companions would have the option to handily create podcasts. Only a PC with essential sight and sound abilities, similar to mouthpiece input, sound yield, and programming to record voice, consolidate with mood melodies and convert to low quality and little size MP3 position. At that point, you need only an FTP to represent transferring the MP3s. A piece of fundamental information about RSS 2.0 gauges is additionally required. For this last choice, you can utilize currently accessible feeds and change them for your own needs. I just began utilizing this strategy, as learning RSS 2.0 necessities times. I replicated a previously made RSS record and altered it dependent on my own needs, and it worked without having enough information. To download your podcasts, the customer ought to introduce extremely fundamental aggregator programming, one like iPodder, which is free. Lastly, an MP3 player programming like iTunes or Microsoft Media Player is as of now introduced on Windows operating systems.

Podcasting, similar to weblogging, is quickly developing and consistently, new podcasts in various fields, from verse to technology, from preparing to radio channels are being made and distributed on the Internet. Some unique directories and websites list podcasts and podcasting websites. You can begin from one of these directories and arrive at hundreds and thousands of accessible and known podcasts on the Internet. One of these directories is which has arranged podcasts in a catalog structure. It could be a decent beginning point for your experience.

Things to Consider Before Starting Your Podcast

Podcasting can be a lot of fun. Through it, you can get your message out to a large number of people who will enjoy listening to you and what you have to say on your "internet radio show."

Podcasting can also be a lot of work. Before you get started with your show, and possibly end up over your head, here are six simple things that you should consider.

Passion. You need to make sure that you're talking about your passion or something that you're passionate about. The reason for this is to help you stay motivated and continue producing episodes on those days that you have the "I don't wanna." An easy test for your passion is this: Can you come up with 50 different things related to the topic you want to talk about?

Schedule. With what frequency will you be podcasting? Once you pick a schedule, stick to it. Once a day requires a huge commitment, once a month is not frequent enough, once a week is ideal. If you could come up with 50 different things to talk about (see #1 above), then you essentially have one year's worth of topics for your show.

Blogging. Many of the same principles that apply to blog apply to produce your show. Like with blogging, your goal should be to increase your subscribers. To accomplish that, make sure that you are providing good content and getting feedback on your content to make sure that you're on topic.

Hosting. Ideally, you should host your files yourself on your server instead of hosting the files on someone else's. By hosting the files yourself, you avoid inconvenienced should that third party go out of business. The biggest con to hosting the files yourself is that it takes some time and a little technical expertise to setup your hosting.

Syndication. This refers to how you will distribute your podcast. People need to be able to subscribe to your show, so you need to pick a syndication platform that will make this easy for your listeners. The iTunes music store, Podcast Pickle, etc. are examples of places where you can syndicate your content.

Money. Are you planning on monetizing, or in other words, are you planning to make money from your podcast? I posit that you should not worry about making money from the get-go, but rather grow into making money as your audience grows. Whether you plan to sell ads or sell affiliate products, make sure that you have a plan for how you are going to make money from your podcast when that time comes.

At the very least, you should address these issues before you start podcasting. There are many other tasks, such as growing your audience, growing your subscribers, finding guests, etc. that you may need to consider as well.

Podcasting Software

Podcasting has progressed significantly from its introduction to the world in 2003. In somewhat less than a year from that point forward, Podcasting had gotten well known the world over, with more and more information accessible to everybody. Presently, you can barely locate a solitary individual who hasn't in any event known about the word podcast.

More than simply searching for podcasts and tuning in to them, the intriguing activity for some is to make their podcasts. There is unquestionably no need for information on the most proficient method to cause your own to the podcast. Podcasting is very basic - all you need is you and your material and the privilege podcasting programming. There is a plethora of podcasting programming to be found on the web. Here are some important hints to recall while picking the one for you.

First, you need to get a sound recorder. There is a lot of sound recorders out there. What you have to search for is programming that records quality sound. You need to ensure it runs with your working framework.

At that point, locate a decent sound editor. Recordings consistently should be altered to introduce the best quality podcast. Some product consolidates recording and altering highlights. These sorts of programming will make it simpler for you.

In picking your recording and altering programming, observe its yield format. For the most part, the MP3 format gives you the best similarity for sound, while MPEG is best for video. On the off chance that the product you pick doesn't make these sorts of records, you can utilize transformation programming. It is important for your transformation programming to have the option to pack your record to a reasonable size. Littler document sizes are simpler to transfer and download.

Before you distribute your podcast, utilize playback programming. You will have the option to tune in to your podcast similarly as subscribers will. This will guarantee the nature of your last item.

In picking podcasting programming, you ought to likewise check on the off chance that it makes RSS channels. Podcasts are found and downloaded by clients through RSS channels. Without this ability, you would need to locate your own RSS channel creator.

Maybe probably the ideal approaches to advance your podcast would be through iTunes. In this way, it would be extraordinary in addition to if your podcasting programming made substantial iTunes takes care of. Along these lines, your podcast would have the most extreme introduction. More audience members will have the option to get to your podcast. More potential audience members will get some answers concerning your podcast.

To transfer your podcast, you need a record move program. There are sure podcasting programming that naturally incorporates this element. It is useful for you to utilize programming offering such usefulness.

Without advancement, you should distribute your podcast. Programming that permits posting in podcast directories gives you an edge. Most podcast audience members search for new podcasts in the various directories on the web. Try not to permit your podcast to stay unnoticed by passing up the directories.

Podcasts are to make an arrangement. Updates to your arrangement are a piece of podcasting. Pick programming that will caution different directories for refreshes. Like this, you won't need to physically alarm every directory you recorded in.

How to Choose a Podcast Publishing Platform

Creating and distributing a podcast requires not just recording and transferring sound documents to a web server, yet additionally getting a web nearness for the podcast. As a component of it is additionally producing a podcast feed for the podcasts.

This entire procedure may appear to be confused; however, if you experience it by and by, it isn't as troublesome as it sounds. Add to the way that corrects now, and there are a ton of coordinated podcast distributing platform to look over. It ought to be effortless and simple.

Most importantly, there are various sorts of podcast facilitating platforms. The most widely recognized one is a run of the mill web facilitating platform. A blog programming can be introduced on this server to transform it into the point and snap podcast distributing platform.

A coordinated platform, for example, in podcast facilitating administration, incorporates blog programming with circle space and data transfer capacity, in addition to other things. The more modern platform likewise incorporates measurements that are important for podcast promotion.

A podcast distributing platform includes three primary parts:

1. Podcast record the board

Any web server ought to give in any event one approach to transfer and oversee records. The most widely recognized is through File Transfer Protocol (FTP), or electronic record director, WebDAV document framework, or incorporated record administrator that accompanies blog programming.

2. Podcast site and page the executives

Any web distributing platform will do this. However, a blog comprehends the issues and shields you from taking care of HTML codes. On the off chance that you realize how to utilize email, you know more than enough to distribute a podcast scene page utilizing a blog.

Another advantage of a blog as a distributing platform is that it is naturally filed, listed by blog web crawlers, and incorporates an inner conversation for singular posts just as remotely through trackback.

3. Podcast feed age

The last piece of a podcast distributing platform is for producing podcast-perfect feed. Utilizing blog programming, this procedure is programmed. Numerous bloggers don't have a clue about that they are creating a feed with their blog, yet this is the way into each podcast.

For this explanation, the blog has become the most mainstream podcast distributing platform. With a single tick blog,the establishment includes on most facilitating accounts; presently, everybody can assemble a podcast blog, no problem at all.

From that point forward, as a podcaster, you should simply be transferring the podcast document, composing scene notes, and determine the record you need to encase as a podcast. Snap distribute, and you are finished distributing the notes and the podcast feed.

Ten Simple Steps to Setting Up Your First Podcast

As a business proprietor or expert, you'll be searching for ways for viable and savvy approaches to growing your business. Podcasting is a superb method to advance your business or give increased the value of your customers. They can assist you with building your rundown of effectively intrigued adherents and upgrade your expert notoriety and authority inside your field.

Right now, be giving you how you can cause an expert level to the podcast in ten straightforward strides without waiting to be a PC wizard.

We should start with a short clarification of a podcast.

A podcast is just a computerized media audio record (called an MP3 document) or video document that is accessible on the web for downloading and playback on a cell phone, for example, an iPod or another MP3 player, PC, tablet or PC. This adaptability permits the audience to tune in to a podcast any place they pick - at home while voyaging or to grind away. Knowing this, you can make content that is proper to the various conditions or parts of an audience's way of life.

There are numerous programs accessible that will assist you with creating a podcast, yet for our model, we are going to utilize the most well known, that is, soundcard.com. When you've picked up commonality with the procedure, glance around at different alternatives that intrigue you.

So how about we begin!

Stage 1: First, you'll have to watch that your audio or potential video record is in MP3 design. The chance that the record isn't in MP3 design, at that point, utilize a document converter. You should simply utilize explicit programming, which permits you to change over and encode sound records on PC and Mac. It's exceptionally speedy and simple to do, so don't be put off if this is the thing that you have to do.

Utilize your web index to run an inquiry on something like "document changing over mp3," and a rundown of free or business programming suppliers will lead you to the correct decision for you. Inside a couple of moments of starting, you'll have the option to transform your substance into a suitable document type.

On the off chance that your audio/video record is all set at that point to move onto stage 2.

Stage 2: Set up a FREE record at soundcloud.com

Soundcloud's free record has capacity limits, yet once you arrive at your breaking point, you can update for a little expense. Setting up a record is a fast and basic procedure with clear directions to take you through each stride. It took under 5 minutes to set up my record and complete my profile.

As you're creating podcasts for expert and business reasons, make a username which mirrors your image effectively and incorporate your photograph or organization logo picture for your profile. It's best similarly as with everything internet based life, to up an alternate record for increasingly close to home material.

When your record is dynamic, transfer your MP3 (that is, adhere to directions that permit the document to be duplicated from the PC onto their server). When the MP3 transferred, verify that you make the document open, downloadable and that you balanced the settings with the goal that you have enacted it for gadgets.

No issues up until now. presently for stage three

Stage 3: If you don't have a blog as of now, you can go to a website like blogger.com and arrange a free blog/podcast account. When you have actuated your record, you're prepared to start posting. Presently we have to connect your audio document to your blog with the goal that it shows up as another post.

Stage 4: If you're utilizing blogger, to start posting click on "Start Posting," at that point, click "Settings," and afterward click "Organizing." Once under the designing tab search for the "Show Link Field," ensure this field is set to "Yes" and spare the settings.

Stage 5: Now click on the "Posting" tab to come back to the blog, and afterward click on "Include another post." Once under "Include another post," give the post a title, and afterward, glue in the URL connect for the podcast from Soundcloud in the "Connection" box.

Here you can likewise compose a portrayal of the podcast in the primary body of your post - remember to utilize solid catchphrases to take advantage of your website streamlining (SEO) potential. At the point when no doubt about it, "Distribute."

For WordPress, contingent upon your format, you ought to have the option to see symbols by the container where you would type in another section. By the symbols, you should see "transfer/embed." Select either audio or video relying upon the document you need to add to your blog.

For the last stages, we have to set up the feed for your podcast with the goal that individuals can buy into it. Once more, it's a basic procedure, and I've picked famous assistance called feedburner.com to do this.

Stage 6: Go to feedburner.com and either arrange another record (if you've Google account use it to sign in).

Stage 7: Once you've signed in, glue the URL from your blog entry into the "Consume A Feed Right This Instant" segment; at that point, click "I'm a podcaster," and afterward click "Next."

Stage 8: Now, you need to give your feed a title and address; at that point, click "Next." Once more, to benefit as much as possible from this SEO opportunity, guarantee you've utilized the solid and important watchwords. When you've presented this data, it can't be changed, so put in no time flat considering what you type.

Stage 9: That's it; your podcast feed is presently live and prepared for download. All around done! Be that as it may, before you've completed, there's only one final significant advance to finish.

Stage 10: By guaranteeing your podcast procedure is iTunes well disposed, you'll permit your audience to choose your substance from one of the world's biggest assets. Surely, there is a desire that your podcast will be accessible through this outlet.

To get that going, simply click "Next" on the Congratulations page. This screen will permit you to pick a few choices that will make your podcast iTunes amicable - click "Next" when done. This screen will likewise let you track distinctive details from your podcast and merits setting.

Very much done, you've set up your podcast in ten stages!

In around thirty minutes, you furnished yourself with the apparatuses you have to share your podcast with a worldwide audience. To include more scenes essentially follow the above advances once more, however as there's no compelling reason to set up another record, simply sign in. Remember, your feed address is the location set in Step 8.

How to Choose a Topic For Your Podcast

For podcasters who produce a podcast as an approach to broaden their message and arrive at the objective market, maybe this isn't an issue by any stretch of the imagination. In any case, for individuals who need to begin a podcast as a free distributing adventure or as a side interest, this might be confounding. It happens to us all at a certain stage. Regardless of whether to follow enthusiasm or cash, how to decide whether your energy produced, etc.

One potential and simple approach to begin your examination are by perusing through web journals and podcast destinations or indexes to perceive what areas of now there. Even though you can't discover unequivocally how they bring in cash from podcasting, in any event, you can perceive what topics are mainstream and if the podcasters have applied adaptation models. If one adaptation methodology is normal among numerous podcasters, you should realize that maybe it is a feasible model for different podcasts as well.

How would you decide the topic for your podcast? Here are a few inquiries to kick you off.

1. What is your obsession?

Guaranteeing gainfulness from a business, you are going to manufacture it significantly. We don't need a business that follows our enthusiasm yet won't bolster us monetarily.

Then again, podcasting requires a ton of direct associations with the topic. You will discover at one point in the business that it is extremely difficult to push ahead, and you need to drive yourself to do the scene. This happens to us all, even the individuals who are near progress. Energy, as a rule, kicks in at this circumstance. While you accomplish something you are enthusiastic about, it is, to a lesser extent, a task, and you are bound to complete it.

2. Is the topic well known?

You need to offset your energy with an advertising request. It is the main way you can guarantee productivity.

You need to gauge that the topic you picked is on request. One approach to decide this is to look into the accessibility of items in the market. Discover destinations and magazines individuals in your specialty showcase peruse and visit. Likewise, dive into catchphrase examine apparatuses. What they go into web crawlers to discover data and items identified with your specialty?

3. How might you get to potential audience members?

Since you have coordinate a topic with your energy, you should decide methods for which you can get to the potential audience members.

The inquiry is, "How might you get to them, proficiently?"

By proficient, I imply that offering access to the audience members, regardless of how costly it is, you should have the option to get positive, quantifiable profit. Much the same as publicizing, you need to, in any event, make back the initial investment toward the front and afterward benefit from the recurrent deals. Having a sound system that coordinates with the podcast is significant right now.

4. Will you have enough to state?

Content is the backbone of each podcast. Do you have enough to state that you could create content on a predictable reason for quite a long time or years?

Of course, you can utilize many substance age strategies like meeting different specialists or tirade about the news;

however, one thing for certain is that you, despite everything, must have some unique substance. Be that as it may, that you need to be a specialist in a specific topic, do you have enough to the state to set up your status?

5. What is your adaptation model?

Are there enough pay streams to help your podcast? With all the notoriety and traffic, would you be able to discover approaches to bring home the bacon straightforwardly from it or to use other roundabout techniques?

After investing some energy with those inquiries, right now is an ideal opportunity to begin podcasting. Keep in mind, while it is pleasant to have enthusiasm around a topic which hasa tremendous interest and low to direct rivalries, in actuality, only sometimes do we unearth such a topic.

Attempt not to let this get you down, however. Each specialty will have its shortcomings. For whatever length of time that you know about them, you can work to beat them. On the off chance that a podcast isn't reasonable for your specialty, locate another.

On the off chance that it is your business you are advancing through a podcast, there are constantly other promoting channels.

The key is to, at any rate, make it truly conceivable to benefit from the specialty before you bounce in. Along these lines, invest as a lot of energy varying and don't hurry through the procedure.

It is harmless to say that you are driving boatloads of traffic from internet-based life? You should.

Creating A Podcast

Creating a podcast is both basic and fun, and with a limited quantity of exertion, it can result in both yourself and your audience members. A podcast is essentially a media document, which has transferred to the Internet and is syndicated out to audience members, a significant number of whom are ideally endorsers, for playback on their PCs or MP3 players. The word podcast can likewise allude to the strategy by which the media documents syndicated out to audience members.

When recording an audio podcast, the show ought to recorded in the most excellent conceivable. Truly outstanding and general basic, programs out there for audio recording and altering is Audacity; incidentally, it is additionally free. In the wake of recording, you should send out your audio into the MP3 position, which has become the standard for podcasts, even though there are many podcasts accessible in WMV (Windows Media) design moreover. In any case, sending out your podcast in something besides the MP3 arrangement may imply that a few clients won't have the option to tune in to your podcasts.

While creating your MP3, you should remember the accompanying about quality. A 64k piece rate is extraordinary for talk radio, audiobooks, talk radio with ambient melodies, and pretty much whatever else you can consider. Be that as it may, that you are determined to distributing quality music, if you are stating a musician or DJ, at that point, you ought to firmly consider distributing your substance in a 128k piece rate.

There are likewise podcasters who decide to incorporate ID3 labels. The most now and again utilized ones are the title (the title of the show) and artist (for the most part, the podcaster), even though I have seen podcasters likewise incorporate classification, year, and even remarks. This is anything but a poorly conceived notion, particularly if you are a musician, yet in addition to the individuals who may spare their podcasts.

In the wake of creating your audio media, you should transfer it to your site for appropriation.

Next comes the assignment of creating the RSS (Really Simple Syndication) channel. An RSS channel contains all the required data about your podcast and focuses forthcoming audience members to both your site and to your facilitated audio records on the Internet. Some podcasters make their feeds by hand; however, for some individuals, this is a genuinely troublesome errand to embrace. There are many free choices accessible on the Internet for creating your podcast feed. However, I would suggest FeedForAll, a quality program that can be downloaded at an unobtrusive cost, accessible at. Not exclusively do these programs help you appropriately group your RSS channel, which is basic, with the goal that everybody might have the option to understand it; however, they likewise disentangle the whole procedure.

One of the significant missteps I see with podcasts is that numerous podcasters neglect to give definite portrayals to their podcast arrangement and individual shows. Tragically very frequently, numerous podcasters may incorporate just a couple of words or no depiction at all for their arrangement or shows. This is a significant selling point for your podcast and ought not to ignore; commonly, this is the main possibility that a podcaster should sell their podcast to potential audience members.

The podcast arrangement depiction ought to be brief yet enlightening, containing 75-100 words (roughly 4-5 full sentences), and should give your audience members the substance of what the podcast arrangement is about.

Data, for example, the host's name, any qualifications, and when and how frequently the podcast is refreshed, are on the whole critical to incorporate.

Thing portrayals, or depictions of individual shows, ought to be point by point about the show. It isn't important to incorporate data about the whole show, however, ought to consistently contain data on, in any event, the first 50% of the show. Numerous fruitful podcasters thing portrayals are just a transcript of their verbal introduction toward the start of the show. The thing portrayal ought to likewise be roughly 75-100 words, and ought to contain talking focuses for the show, music line-up, or other pertinent data. It is moreover imperative to take note of that the thing portrayal for a show can likewise contain HTML coding, permitting you to make hyperlinks or incorporate pictures.

Another significant part of creating your RSS channel is to remember an IMAGE component for your channel; even though it isn't required for the usefulness of your RSS channel, it is just about a need. Numerous podcasters call this album art or a spread; it is critical for marking purposes.

In the wake of wrapping up your RSS channel and sparing it, you ought to transfer the channel to your site.

At long last, it is dependent upon you to get your feed out onto the Internet. Distributing the feed on your landing page isn't sufficient. You should set aside the effort to list your podcast in a few podcast directories/entrances.

Can You Start A Podcast With No Money?

With the technology accessible today, you can start a podcast without going through any money whatsoever and have it distributed to the world by this evening! Truly, it is that simple to do.

You needn't bother with any extravagant hardware, no altering programming, not by any means an extravagant mouthpiece!

Extremely, all you need is an intriguing subject of which you have more information than the normal individual. That is it!

You shouldn't be a researcher that trains the subject at an Ivy League college. You just need to have more information on that theme than the normal individual.

Be that as it may, you must not start a podcast because it is the "cool thing" to do at this moment. You ought not to start a podcast because your companions are doing it. You ought not to start a podcast on the off chance that you are just going to pitch your items to bring in some money from it (individuals will see directly through that)!

In vindictiveness of the fact that it is genuinely simple and cheap to start a podcast, getting individuals to tune in and follow (buy-in) to your podcast is a unique ball game (which will examine in an alternate article).

It is significant for you to know precisely what a podcast is.

In its essential structure, a podcast is just an audio document, produced using an account, and stacked to a stage that is open to your audience using the Internet. That is all it is.

I started my first podcast by talking into flip-style wireless (I'm maturing myself presently, right?). The sound quality seemed like I was talking into flip-style wireless, as well!

Be that as it may, cutting edge PDAs have progressed up until now, numerous individuals can't tell on the off chance that you recorded into your mobile phone or a mouthpiece. The technology accessible today is surprising!

In the incident that you truly need to get extravagant, get an amplifier or mouthpiece/headset mix that will plug into your phone. This will do in propelling the nature of your account too. What's more, that combo framework is under $50 (much of the time).

Yet, to return to my primary concern, you can get an extraordinary sounding audio document utilizing just your wireless, with zero out-of-pocket dollars.

On the off chance that you record utilizing your mobile phone, you can utilize an application from Anchor.FM that will permit you to transfer the document straightforwardly to them. They will, at that point, handle the conveyance to the major podcast directories for you. Your documents are in a flash accessible around the globe!

To transfer your audio records to Apple Podcasts (and most significant directories), you ought to make what is known as "spread art" for your podcast.

There are free places online that will permit you to make this spread art. I like to utilize Canva.com (and it has a free form to utilize).

To present your podcast to Apple Podcasts (which, coincidentally, is THE significant player in podcasting directories), you should make your spread art within any event a 3000 x 3000-pixel square picture. Just JPEG or PNG documents ought to make, as these will quite often be acknowledged. Other record types may not be endorsed.

What's more, don't attempt to make an honor winning spread art picture. Something as straightforward as your name or the name of the podcast on a shading foundation would be adequate.

An excess of "hecticness" would divert from your spread art. You need individuals to have the option to rapidly look at, recognize, and recall your spread art. An excessive amount of data won't permit them to do that.

That state, don't stress a lot over "the ideal podcast name." I prescribe to my customers that the name ought to be short (presumably not more than 4-5 words), snappy (for example, something that portrays the podcast, podcast theme or audience) and simple to recollect.

I have a few podcasts. However, I'll utilize my podcast question and answer program, for instance. My program is designated, "Ask Bob Podcasting Q&A" - it says everything in that spot! Individuals "ask me" (Bob) inquiries concerning podcasting, and I answer them on the podcast (Podcasting Q&A). Simple, isn't that so?

There you have the rudiments of beginning.

In synopsis, use what you as of now have without going through any money.

Utilize the free forms of a podcast have (like Anchor.FM) and to make your spread art (like Canva.com).

Take a piece to make a short, appealing, illustrative name that mentions to everybody what your podcast is about.

At that point, share it with the world!

Can You Make Money Podcasting?

Podcasting has become a famous route for websites and blog proprietors to spread their data and feelings on the web. Podcasting should be possible in either a just audio configuration or in a video group with audio, which can likewise, at times, alluded to as a webcast. As more individuals get on board with the fleeting podcasting trend, a few people are in any event, attempting to bring in money from their podcasts. For the individuals who are considering podcasting or in any event, for the individuals who as of now have one going, the inquiry is: Can money truly be made online by podcasting?

Indeed, money can be made online through podcasting and here are a couple of the most mainstream approaches to doing this:

Regardless of whether in audio or video position, a podcast should set up on a site. Web journals are a famous alternative for facilitating an audio document or webcast. Because of this, huge numbers of similar money-making strategies that blog proprietors, as of now use, can likewise be utilized with podcasting. This implies podcasters can set up publicizing on their websites or online journals to bring in money.

Another strategy for bringing in money with podcasting is by advancing an organization or brand during the genuine podcast itself. To do this, an organization must contact the podcaster and request that they advance their site, organization, or administrations for a charge or the podcaster may get in touch with certain organizations that the person feels may be keen on having their organization referenced during the podcast.

Many podcasts request gifts to keep their podcasts going. Setting up a video or audio document takes time, and money and podcasters need to pay for gear and webspace or to continue onward. Remember, in any case, that while you can bring in money podcasting through gifts, this strategy ought not to be utilized to make easy money or to pay for individual costs. On the off chance that tolerant gifts for the podcast, the individual ought to make the best decision and utilize those assets to pay for what it expenses to keep the podcast going.

How To Create Your First Podcast

This book will clarify the rudiments. In straightforward terms, podcasting originates from two words, the case for iPod and broadcasting. It's astounding what an ordinary individual with a PC can do. Much the same as blogging, you can make a podcast about your preferred leisure activity, or intrigue.

1. There are four apparatuses that you will require: a PC, an amplifier, headset (discretionary), and recording programming. It would help if you recorded in the mp3 group. A free account programming program that I would prescribe is Audacity. That you have never utilized chronicle programming, there are instructional exercises on the Audacity site. You can likewise discover instructional practices on YouTube.

2. There is an expectation to absorb information, so explore different avenues regarding a couple of preliminary runs. Record for a moment or two, and play it back. How can it sound? You needn't bother with an expensive amplifier to get a fair chronicle. What you would prefer not to hear is low volume, twisting, or foundation

commotions coming through. If there is an issue, make the vital acclimations to your chronicle programming. How agreeable would you say you were behind the amplifier? Did you freeze up? Tune in to how often you hack, or state "uh."

3. When recording your podcast, would it be a good idea for you to utilize content? There are a few ways of thinking concerning the material on the off chance that your perusing from the content. It may sound exhausting. It would help if you had the option to ad-lib. Rather than content, you may be progressively happy with utilizing a diagram. Make a rundown of talking focuses; this will help keep your musings composed. In any case, you don't need a lot of "um" and "uhs" all through your account.

4. When recording your podcast, you should incorporate a couple of components. In the first place, your podcast will require a pleasant presentation message. Quickly present yourself, or your organization, and clarify what the program will be about. Presently you're prepared to record the body of your message. At long last, you will need to include an end explanation toward the finish of

the program. You can advise your audience members when you're going to discharge your next podcast, and what it will be about. In the case of nothing else, you can say a straightforward farewell and say thanks to them for tuning in.

5. You will likewise require a few methods for conveying your podcast. Since you have spared your podcast to an mp3 record, basically transfer it to your site. At that point, you might need to think about starting one. The other option is to present your program to a free podcast facilitating site. Utilize your preferred web index to locate a "free podcast facilitating" website.

If you have a comment, I urge you to take a stab at podcasting Whether for entertainment only or to bring in money, and podcasting permits you to contact an engaged and faithful audience effectively. There is an expectation to absorb information, yet you can discover most answers only utilizing your preferred internet searcher. Have a fabulous time, and let yourself heard.

How to Make a Podcast Interactive

Podcasts are an incredibly useful asset for promoting and building up notoriety. Be that as it may, they have one shortcoming. They aren't intuitive.

Getting your audience associated with your podcast requires some component of intuitiveness. They should be part of the podcast to have a stake in it. Be that as it may, podcasts are pre-recorded, so how might you include your audience?

Right now, demonstrating how to cause a to podcast intuitive. While you can't cause a to podcast intuitive straightforwardly - that would include a live podcast - you can cause it to seem intelligent. Since a live podcast is a logical inconsistency in wording, try to incorporate postponed live collaborations. Here are four models:

1. Continuously request messages, remarks, and questions.

Regardless of what you train, it's constantly a smart thought to request questions. Nobody is going to comprehend what you have educated during a podcast. On the off chance that they do, at that point, you most likely shouldn't have made the podcast so far-reaching in any case. Questions do not just assist you with expanding the intelligence of your podcast, but on the other hand, they're an extraordinary wellspring of points and statistical surveying. The best spot to find new subjects and related items is to ask your client base. On account of a podcast, that implies your audience.

2. Have an "Our audience members ask" segment.

This is the opposite side of the inquiry and messages. You have a section design podcast you ought to consistently - perhaps should - have an "Our audience members ask" segment. This segment will permit you to respond to addresses your audience has asked - or ought to have inquired. Regardless of whether you make them up yourself!

3. Have a recorded Q and A meeting.

While the podcast itself can't really be live and still be a podcast, there's no explanation it can't be recorded live. One of the methods you can use to build intelligence is to record a live inquiry and answer meeting. This is a teleseminar in which your audience and clients can bring in and pose inquiries. Consequently, you'll put forth a valiant effort to address those inquiries. An instructing call is an incredible hotspot for this as your training customers are now prepared to pose inquiries.

4. Have an audience meet the host.

One of the incredible strategies for creating a podcast is to meet a specialist. Yet, what occurs on the off unintended that you turn that around. Consider the possibility that you are being met. The transitory host will be seen as somebody who is on a similar level as your audience. It will be as though they were talking with you. The outcome will be an intelligent chronicle. Rapidly and simple!

How to Make Your Podcast Newsworthy

Journalists want to profile new and exciting stories, and podcasters are continually trying to find publicity. Then why aren't more podcasters being profiled in magazines, newspapers, and radio or television programs? It's everything to try to with what podcasters determine is newsworthy.

Here are just a couple of announcements that some podcasters claim is newsworthy:

Releasing a podcast

Releasing a replacement episode of a podcast that hasn't been updated in months

Releasing the 20th episode of a podcast

Being listed in iTunes

Saying that some unknown (or even known) person appeared as a guest on a podcast

Going from 30-minutes to 15-minutes

Getting some celebrity to supply your bumper

Moving from mono to stereo output

Using a high definition microphone rather than just a mic

Just because your podcast is now shorter, sounds better, features someone, and is listed somewhere isn't newsworthy. All this hype about the frequency, sound, and format of your podcast is merely adding noise to the eternal clutter that permeates cyberspace.

Instead, tie within the launch of your podcast to a special event, holiday, or current item. For example:

A chiropractor can launch a series of episodes that specialize in common back problems children experience thanks to oversize backpacks. This chiropractor can time the launch with the rear to high school season. This is often an example of tying within the start of your podcast with a special event.

A career coach can launch a couple of episodes that specialize in work-at-home strategies during a city full transit strike. This is often an example of tying within the launch of your podcast with a current item.

A company that produces paper cups can launch a couple of episodes that provide recommendations on the way to steel oneself against the Christmas holiday. This is often an example of tying within the launch of your podcast with a vacation.

If you time the launch of your podcast with a special event, holiday, or current news items, you will find that you're going to attract the media interview effortlessly. Let your competitors make the error of releasing press releases that announce their use of a replacement microphone. Instead, transcend your format, frequency, and sound and make your podcast relevant to journalists so that they will write a story about it.

Podcast Like A Pro

It's the primary commemoration of the Work Alchemy podcast! I'm so charmed to have presented to you these moving and inside and out discussions with business visionaries and pioneers who consolidate customary business accomplishment with truly having any kind of effect on the planet.

More than anything that is the thing that I need for you: monetary achievement + positive commitment = IMPACT. In the podcast, you can figure out how these business people and pioneers did it. What's more, I'm anticipating about bringing you more!

I've taken in a great deal en route, and need to impart it to you, so you can make your master level podcast. Think about this article as Podcasting 201. For the rudiments, look at What You Need to Know To Start Your Podcast.

The uplifting news is, you needn't bother with an expert studio or many elevated level professionals to support you. Podcasting like a professional is open to each entrepreneur with even ostensible assets.

Here are eight methodologies to up the nature of your podcast to expert level:

1. Make a considerable accumulation

On the off chance that there's one thing I've taken in, it's to make a noteworthy excess of scenes. On the off chance that you're communicating week by week, at that point, I prescribe at any rate a month ahead. It's inescapable that meetings should be rescheduled, and significant undertakings may back you off in making new scenes. At the point when you make an excess, you'll settle on better and lower-stress choices about everything to do with the podcast, from topic to specialized contemplations. Besides, your crowd will cherish the consistency.

2. Shock individuals

Once your podcast is fully operational for some time, the curiosity begins to wear off. Regardless of whether your topic or subject keeps on drawing in individuals, give individuals a valid justification to tune in to new scenes by blending it up.

If your podcast is only you, at that point, acquire a few visitors for a board or meeting. Do lady in-the-road meets on your topic at an occasion (so you can control sound quality).

If your podcast is a progression of meetings, at that point, get your viewpoint with only you as the host and visitor. As I've found with my podcast, individuals need to hear your point of view!

3. Offer various lengths

Your audience members don't generally have the opportunity to tune in to that full brief meeting, regardless of whether it was intriguing. Give individuals an assortment of lengths to tune in to, so they can pick a shorter scene if their time is constrained.

Some podcasts have a characterized or predictable shorter length. While that can make it simpler to tune in, there's additionally a breaking point to how profound you can go with a subject. Settle on a decision about whether you are going for straightforwardness or profundity. That will rely upon who your audience members are.

4. Tune in to your audience members

Think about your topic and your crowd. It merits finding good pace audience members and their inclinations. You can request that individuals give you input on your podcast, either from your email list or on the podcast itself. Web-based life is an extraordinary method to realize what your audience members need. I've gotten such a lot of significant criticism that way.

5. Connect with audience members from the principal minute

The prologue to your podcast is significant. Compose it with the goal that it catches your crowd's consideration immediately. Use it to establish the pace and convey significant data about what's to come.

Regardless of whether individuals have been tuning in for some time, various parts of a commonplace presentation will fly into their mindfulness each time they hear it. Thus, make the most of each word.

6. Incorporate a source of inspiration

Most podcasts aren't adapted straightforwardly, so remember a convincing source of inspiration for your podcast. Consider how the podcast fits into your general showcasing and business system. Remembering how the podcast can impact your business, what source of inspiration will serve that best at present? Requesting that individuals join your email list, offering an item or administration, or welcoming them to an occasion is, for the most part, prospects.

7. Be cautious about how you adapt

You can likewise adapt your podcast all the more legitimately. Some podcasts are adapted by publicizing, or through corporate or establishment subsidizing. In these cases, express the publicizing or subsidizing in each scene, to give individuals an away from where the financing originates from. That is an authentic method to keep your podcast proceeding to try and furnish you with some salary to make it.

I've adapted as of late of a podcast that charges individuals by the scene to be on it. The proprietor is utilizing their enormous crowd to permit individuals to pick up the introduction. Remember, however, that many podcasts with enormous crowds are searching for visitors that don't need to pay.

Another strategy I've seen is to utilize this paid way to deal with being in a roundabout way associated with the celebrated by affiliation. An expression of alert: to keep up the trust of your crowd, don't misdirect your kin about who you podcast "with" in these paid courses of action. It could well blowback on you on the off chance that you are discovered.

Outside of this handy thought, I could never advocate misdirecting individuals. Be mindful so as not to undermine your believability with faulty strategies. When trust is lost, it's difficult to recapture. Make your item or administration extraordinary and build up a connection with the network, and you won't need to forfeit your honesty to be fruitful.

8. Assist individuals with finding the pieces

Pulling out the incredible minutes in your podcast will attract your crowd alternately and appealingly. Send them an email with podcast chunks, as I have done, or make isolated, a lot shorter scenes with features from the full account. That way, individuals can simply fly in and still profit by the key focuses.

I've even increased this methodology with my interpretation of what my visitors have stated, to include esteem. The entirety of that can be conveyed in a minimal bundle of time that makes it simple for your crowd to peruse or tune in.

Podcasting has become increasingly more well known as a path for individuals to advance their organizations. Help yours stand apart from this undeniably packed road of permeability by offering an expert methodology, one you can be pleased with, and that fits into your general procedure.

Ten Simple Steps to Setting Up Your First Podcast

As a business proprietor or expert, you'll be searching for ways for viable and savvy approaches to growing your business. Podcasting is a superb method to advance your business or give increased the value of your customers. They can assist you with building your rundown of effectively intrigued adherents and upgrade your expert notoriety and authority inside your field.

Right now, be giving you how you can cause an expert level to the podcast in ten straightforward strides without waiting to be a PC wizard.

We should start with a short clarification of a podcast.

A podcast is just a computerized media audio record (called an MP3 document) or video document that is accessible on the web for downloading and playback on a cell phone, for example, an iPod or another MP3 player, PC, tablet or PC. This adaptability permits the audience to tune in to a podcast any place they pick - at home while voyaging or to grind away. Knowing this, you can make content that is proper to the various conditions or parts of an audience's way of life.

There are numerous programs accessible that will assist you with creating a podcast, yet for our model, we are going to utilize the most well known, that is, soundcard.com. When you've picked up commonality with the procedure, glance around at different alternatives that intrigue you.

So how about we begin!

Stage 1: First, you'll have to watch that your audio or potential video record is in MP3 design. The chance that the record isn't in MP3 design, at that point, utilize a document converter. You should simply utilize explicit programming, which permits you to change over and encode sound records on PC and Mac. It's exceptionally speedy and simple to do, so don't be put off if this is the thing that you have to do.

Utilize your web index to run an inquiry on something like "document changing over mp3," and a rundown of free or business programming suppliers will lead you to the correct decision for you. Inside a couple of moments of starting, you'll have the option to transform your substance into a suitable document type.

On the off chance that your audio/video record is all set at that point to move onto stage 2.

Stage 2: Set up a FREE record at soundcloud.com

Soundcloud's free record has capacity limits, yet once you arrive at your breaking point, you can update for a little expense. Setting up a record is a fast and basic procedure with clear directions to take you through each stride. It took under 5 minutes to set up my record and complete my profile.

As you're creating podcasts for expert and business reasons, make a username which mirrors your image effectively and incorporate your photograph or organization logo picture for your profile. It's best similarly as with everything internet based life, to up an alternate record for increasingly close to home material.

When your record is dynamic, transfer your MP3 (that is, adhere to directions that permit the document to be duplicated from the PC onto their server). When the MP3 transferred, verify that you make the document open, downloadable and that you balanced the settings with the goal that you have enacted it for gadgets.

No issues up until now. presently for stage three

Stage 3: If you don't have a blog as of now, you can go to a website like blogger.com and arrange a free blog/podcast account. When you have actuated your record, you're prepared to start posting. Presently we have to connect your audio document to your blog with the goal that it shows up as another post.

Stage 4: If you're utilizing blogger, to start posting click on "Start Posting," at that point, click "Settings," and afterward click "Organizing." Once under the designing tab search for the "Show Link Field," ensure this field is set to "Yes" and spare the settings.

Stage 5: Now click on the "Posting" tab to come back to the blog, and afterward click on "Include another post." Once under "Include another post," give the post a title, and afterward, glue in the URL connect for the podcast from Soundcloud in the "Connection" box.

Here you can likewise compose a portrayal of the podcast in the primary body of your post - remember to utilize solid catchphrases to take advantage of your website streamlining (SEO) potential. At the point when no doubt about it, "Distribute."

For WordPress, contingent upon your format, you ought to have the option to see symbols by the container where you would type in another section. By the symbols, you should see "transfer/embed." Select either audio or video relying upon the document you need to add to your blog.

For the last stages, we have to set up the feed for your podcast with the goal that individuals can buy into it. Once more, it's a basic procedure, and I've picked famous assistance called feedburner.com to do this.

Stage 6: Go to feedburner.com and either arrange another record (if you've Google account use it to sign in).

Stage 7: Once you've signed in, glue the URL from your blog entry into the "Consume A Feed Right This Instant" segment; at that point, click "I'm a podcaster," and afterward click "Next."

Stage 8: Now, you need to give your feed a title and address; at that point, click "Next." Once more, to benefit as much as possible from this SEO opportunity, guarantee you've utilized the solid and important watchwords. When you've presented this data, it can't be changed, so put in no time flat considering what you type.

Stage 9: That's it; your podcast feed is presently live and prepared for download. All around done! Be that as it may, before you've completed, there's only one final significant advance to finish.

Stage 10: By guaranteeing your podcast procedure is iTunes well disposed, you'll permit your audience to choose your substance from one of the world's biggest assets. Surely, there is a desire that your podcast will be accessible through this outlet.

To get that going, simply click "Next" on the Congratulations page. This screen will permit you to pick a few choices that will make your podcast iTunes amicable - click "Next" when done. This screen will likewise let you track distinctive details from your podcast and merits setting.

Very much done, you've set up your podcast in ten stages!

In around thirty minutes, you furnished yourself with the apparatuses you have to share your podcast with a worldwide audience. To include more scenes essentially follow the above advances once more, however as there's no compelling reason to set up another record, simply sign in. Remember, your feed address is the location set in Step 8.

How to Launch a Podcast

The most important thing to think about when launching a podcast is to think about how passionate you're about the topic matter of your podcast. If you are not hooked into your topic, your interest in podcasting about it'll quickly fade.

This is often the way to launch a podcast in 5 steps.

Get a microphone. I'm not talking a $400 studio microphone, but a minimum of something with decent sound capabilities. Do not, under any circumstances, believe your computer's inbuilt mic. Yes, people will persist with a podcast that sounds a touch weak, if the content is spectacular, but not for long. I suggest the Audio-Technical 2020 USB mic (approx. $100 as of this writing) as an honest place to start from. There are many less costly mics out there, just don't use the one in your computer nor one among those long skinny beige ones that you simply get for $5 from the bin at the pc store.

Decide on a schedule. Weekly, monthly, daily, or whenever you are feeling love it. I suggest weekly since most of the people are conversant in that schedule. Whatever you are doing, confirm that you simply stick with your schedule.

Record your podcast. You'll begin with a free application like Audacity, except for a couple of bucks you'll use something more professional like Adobe Audition or Garage Band.

Decide on a distribution network. My suggestion is to use a burning podcast hosting provider. Sure, it costs a touch extra, but tons of normal Webhosting providers don't support hosting your podcast files. Use a devoted or specialized hosting provider like libsyn for hosting your podcast files, and therefore the iTunes music store for distribution to a good audience. iTunes is that the easiest place to host your podcast and is typically the simplest for your listeners to use. Whatever podcast hosting you select, will assist you with uploading the files.

Promote your podcast. Find out who must hear your show, and put it ahead of them. If you've chosen a distribution network wisely, you've also made it easy for people to subscribe to your podcast show, which can make it easy for your audience to grow.

Some may argue that promoting the podcast to a large audience is more important than choosing the content of the show. There's some validity to the present. Some audiences are too small to form them commercially viable.

However, podcasting should be about your passion and not about the dimensions of the audience. It's up to you to decide whether you would like to figure on something solely supported the dimensions of the audience that might hear it, rather than something that you simply hooked in to.

How To Use Podcasting To Build Your Business Online

Broadcast your business using podcasts! A podcast may be a collection of digital media files that are distributed over the web using syndication feeds for repetition. The content is downloaded by users into multiple programs to observed on their computer or portable media device. YouTube has set a precedent for this standard, with nearly 200 million hits per day. The podcast phenomenon has spread worldwide contribution businesses the power to broadcast any idea, and further opportunities to professionally record full segment commercials as marketing tools.

Podcasts are often used for a spread of business needs:

Educational broadcasts or tutorials

New product releases

Product demonstrations

Seminars and training sessions

Internal communications within a corporation or organization

Interviews or news feeds

Company brand introductions

Commentaries

A free deliverable for potential customers

Why are podcasts effective?

When podcasts are wont to communicate internally within a corporation, they will use as a training session for workers or supply corporate updates. Once they use on a corporation website, they will be wont to launch new products as a mini-commercial. Product demonstrations are often wont to build customer relationships, as the customer can choose an RSS feed that might allow customers to receive information automatically, versus having to regularly visit the corporate website. Podcasts are often less costly than traditional advertising, creating a good playing field for giant and little companies to advertise online. They will be created professionally or with software tools on your computer. The media also can be replayed by viewers and forwarded, creating viral marketing potential.

How does one implement?

Step 1: Create an audio file using sound recording software

Audio recording software permits users to record audio files and provides the user with a format that's easy to use and straightforward to implement. Some software to think about would be: Mixcrafts, Text Aloud also Replay Audio.

Step 2: Enhance the audio file to an RSS feed

Start together with your RSS feed provider and enter a title for your podcast alongside an outline of the audio files. You'll get to enter the URL that's related to the feed (often your company home page) and enter the file that contains the audio content, the dimensions of the file, and, therefore, the format. Once you've got entered all of the specified information, you would like to save lots of the FTP file to your server to organize for its launch.

Step 3: Market your podcast

Numerous sites accept podcast submissions, including podcasting stations, podcasts alley, podcast.net, and pocketcasting. Make certain to research each podcast site to work out whether your podcast will meet the submission requirements before submitting it. Your podcast should even be marketed on your website using an RSS feed tool and as a link within your e-zines, e-books, or as a link within your article or blog postings.

Podcasting is a cheap marketing tool for your business and may be used across many business functions to extend business revenues.

Monetizing Your Podcast the Easy Way

Some of you out there have been focusing attempting to make sense of how you could adapt your podcasts, yet trust me, and it isn't as hard as you may suspect. The way to monetizing your podcasts is advertisement space. You know how you tune in to the radio, and the DJ will advance occasions, nearby news, or other data? Well, think about what the radio broadcast is getting paid for that broadcast appointment. Furthermore, those sources that have mentioned that broadcast appointment is known as backers.

Monetizing your podcast works similarly. The main distinction is you are the chief. You find a workable pace pick what kinds of commercials get broadcast appointment, how much time they get, how you will charge for the broadcast appointment, and how you will acknowledge installment for the broadcast appointment. Doesn't that sound extraordinary?

So now you should simply really take care of business. The key thing you need to do is plan out how much time you are eager to use as promotion space. I would propose that you should utilize close to around 2-3 minutes one after another for publicizing. Furthermore, don't believe that you need to do this all at one time since you don't. You could open up with advertisements, you could make a break timespan in the podcast, or you could simply hold out until the end. It is at last up to you.

Next, you would need to give a few, however, concerning what several supporters you will acknowledge at once. Presently this will rely upon the hour of the room that you permit, simply ensure that you remain steady. Additionally, you will need to keep your point of view supports how much space is accessible with the goal that you don't get assaulted.

From that point, you should simply speak with your backers and make original content for the advertisement. Presently this shouldn't belong by any stretch of the imagination. It shouldn't be close to around 1-2 sentences and no more. Also, after this progression, you are prepared to record.

Simply ensure that you adhere to the content and time allotment that you consent to, and you will be okay. Adapt your podcasts can get some significant cash for you, particularly on the off chance that you offer your podcasts for nothing. What's more, remember that your patrons are searching for the best presentation that they can get from you, so consistently put forth a valiant effort to give that.

Top 5 Fool-Proof Ways to Start Monetizing Your New Podcast Business

The time has come to tell you the best way to adapt your Podcasting Business. Focus on the accompanying five Points. Follow just one of the focuses and flawless it, the income you will have produced won't frustrate you.

The podcast is the ideal machine for you to impart your messages to your audience members, move others, and have an effect on your audience members' lives; in any case, you have to transform your Podcast Show into a feasible business that will support itself.

The accompanying focuses are from the littlest income to the most income. Let us make a plunge!

Instructing and tutoring your audience members

As a Podcast Host, you will pick up believability just as prominence and your audience members will find a good pace and trust you, all things considered, they invest energy to tune in to your Podcasts. At the same time, you talk with incredible authority as a host, and that impression of yourself is going to transform into reality every day, while you are developing. Your audience members will need someone they can trust to tutor them.

Training and coaching are extraordinarily amazing for you to begin monetizing your Podcast.

Driving force enrollment for your inward circle individuals

This is the best gathering of your individuals who submit themselves in prevailing with regards to Podcasting, the exceptional individuals who are a piece of a super gathering of individuals, who have outgrown the remainder of the individuals in your local gathering. They are on a more elevated level and expect simply the best from you. This is a choice gathering of individuals who speak with one another and trade thoughts, strategies, data, and significantly more. They are not keen on blending in with the typical individuals, yet they need to connect themselves with these uncommon network individuals. It will be savvy of you to open the entryways like clockwork before you acknowledge any new individuals, to have a live talk with them to check whether they will fit in with the current decision network.

A stunning open door being an Affiliate

In your shows, you are discussing items and administrations that you are utilizing. Thus, you can allude your audience members to your assets page and disclose to them that you are the offshoot of these items and administrations and that it won't cost your audience members a penny to join. Yet, you as the Podcast Host, will get paid and that it will be extremely ground-breaking for your business and that your audience members can give you an immense thank you that way. The audience members truly need to join the offshoots since you will have given them huge amounts of worth.

Leasing reality for your Sponsors

The backers love to support Podcasts because it is an immense profit for their venture for themselves, they will know, that the audience members of your locale will believe you like the Podcast Host. It is a triumphant circumstance, while the patrons realize that you as the Podcast Host will prescribe these items and administrations to your audience members, the audience members realize that you as the Host will confide in the backers. You can offer an instructional exercise and an advantage for your audience members. Your support needs to win, you have to win, yet the greater part of every one of your audience members need to win.

The Number One method for Monetizing your Podcast Business is for you to create your items, administrations, and projects

This is by a long shot the victor of the five different ways to adapt your Podcast Business; different focuses are in a far off second spot.

You may request that how arrive at this stage? The appropriate response is the point at which you are a Podcast Host, you will be going to grow a group of people and that this crowd is going to contact you by sending you an email expressing the amount they appreciated the Podcast and saying thanks to you for a glorious show which implied a great deal to them.

This is your opportunity to exploit those messages, which are gold since individuals are making a special effort to connect with you, and that you can react to by expressing gratitude toward them and asking them what they are battling with? Your crowd will react by enlightening you regarding their agony focuses, hindrances, and difficulties. The ideal open door emerges where you, the Podcast Host, can make an answer and afterward offer the answer for your crowd who have issues with the torment focuses, hindrances, and difficulties. To put it plainly, this is the technique wherein you can adapt monstrously.

Taking everything into account, the main method to adapt your Podcast Business is to realize your audience members' agony focuses, hindrances and difficulties, at that point to make an answer for those and afterward for you to offer the answer for your crowd. Different focuses to consider are: to lease reality to supports, become a partner to all the assets you are utilizing, make a genius enrollment open door for your decision individuals, the instructing and tutoring of your audience members. You will arrive at incredible outcomes by following these focuses.

5 Reasons to Transcribe Your Podcast

Podcasting is the technique for appropriating records, or data (Audio/Video) over the web for the crowd to tune in or see. Frequently Podcasters adapt their podcast by having publicists supporting their show. In any case, numerous Podcasters experience issues monetizing their Podcast following the customary promoting model.

This section discusses five reasons how Podcasters can adapt their podcast by translating.

Following are the best 5 Reasons to Transcribe your podcast and Monetize from them

1. Make your Podcast Transcripts ready to move. Translate your Podcast and make it ready to move. Along these lines, individuals who like to peruse (than to tune in) can purchase your Podcast transcript and read them at recreation.

2. Make your Podcast web crawler (Google/Yahoo/Live) neighborly and be progressively noticeable on the web by translating your Podcasts.

3. A huge number of individuals communicate in English, yet they don't all talk a similar English. English articulation

is very different in various pieces of the world; Cover more extensive crowd by breaking the highlight hindrance, put it in content so anybody on the web from any piece of the world can understand them.

4. Not every person can tune in/hear (hearing weakened) your Podcast, decipher your Podcast and make it accessible to the individuals who much merit.

5. Use organized transcripts installed with standard connections and other showcasing materials for publicizing and adapts your podcasts. This can be your second wellspring of commercial income other than your conventional podcast ad.

How To Use Podcasting To Build Your Business Online

Broadcast your business using podcasts! A podcast may be a collection of digital media files that are distributed over the web using syndication feeds for repetition. The content is downloaded by users into multiple programs to observed on their computer or portable media device. YouTube has set a precedent for this standard, with nearly 200 million hits per day. The podcast phenomenon has spread worldwide contribution businesses the power to broadcast any idea, and further opportunities to professionally record full segment commercials as marketing tools.

Podcasts are often used for a spread of business needs:

Educational broadcasts or tutorials

New product releases

Product demonstrations

Seminars and training sessions

Internal communications within a corporation or organization

Interviews or news feeds

Company brand introductions

Commentaries

A free deliverable for potential customers

Why are podcasts effective?

When podcasts are wont to communicate internally within a corporation, they will use as a training session for workers or supply corporate updates. Once they use on a corporation website, they will be wont to launch new products as a mini-commercial. Product demonstrations are often wont to build customer relationships, as the customer can choose an RSS feed that might allow customers to receive information automatically, versus having to regularly visit the corporate website. Podcasts are often less costly than traditional advertising, creating a good playing field for giant and little companies to advertise online. They will be created professionally or with software tools on your computer. The media also can be replayed by viewers and forwarded, creating viral marketing potential.

How does one implement?

Step 1: Create an audio file using sound recording software

Audio recording software permits users to record audio files and provides the user with a format that's easy to use and straightforward to implement. Some software to think about would be: Mixcrafts, Text Aloud also Replay Audio.

Step 2: Enhance the audio file to an RSS feed

Start together with your RSS feed provider and enter a title for your podcast alongside an outline of the audio files. You'll get to enter the URL that's related to the feed (often your company home page) and enter the file that contains the audio content, the dimensions of the file, and, therefore, the format. Once you've got entered all of the specified information, you would like to save lots of the FTP file to your server to organize for its launch.

Step 3: Market your podcast

Numerous sites accept podcast submissions, including podcasting stations, podcasts alley, podcast.net, and pocketcasting. Make certain to research each podcast site to work out whether your podcast will meet the submission requirements before submitting it. Your podcast should even be marketed on your website using an RSS feed tool and as a link within your e-zines, e-books, or as a link within your article or blog postings.

Podcasting is a cheap marketing tool for your business and may be used across many business functions to extend business revenues.

How to Use Podcasting to Gain Authority For Your Business

Podcasts are maybe one of the most under appraised instruments that you can use to help advance your business. In Part One of this article, I will walk you through precisely what a podcast is and why it is something that you ought to use for your business.

It is obvious nowadays that with the ceaseless advances in technology that we're seeing, the capacity to record and produce a podcast has now become a quite oversimplified task. You never again need a radio station or studio-quality chronicle gear to deliver a decent quality podcast for your audience.

In any case, for what reason do it in any case?

Let's start by taking a gander at precisely what a podcast is. To place it into its least complex terms, a podcast is an audio clasp (or audio document) that can be put (regularly alluded to as installed) anyplace on your site, and can be tuned in to by any individual who visits your site.

Podcasting first got mainstream in 2005 with the dispatch of iTunes. If the most recent insights are to be accepted, and given the present patterns in the deals of convenient media gadgets, upwards of 275 million individuals around the globe will possess a versatile media player constantly 2011.

This reality alone obviously shows the prevalence of tuning in moving, or if nothing else listening when it is advantageous.

So, for what reason is this significant?

For possibilities or clients who are keen on the audio that you have delivered, it can likewise downloaded onto an mp3 media gadget or a PC. Moreover, there is likewise the likelihood that individuals might need to buy into your podcasts. As you'll discover in Part Two of this article, this is something that can give gigantic potential achievement and open doors for your business.

So, one basic motivation behind why podcasts offer such potential advantages for your business is by downloading it, and your audience can process your podcast at a helpful time to them.

This is a significant qualification since it fits in superbly inside the new 'authorization showcasing' structure that I have referenced in past articles. If you can utilize a media (for example, podcasting) that your intended interest group is utilizing and is alright with, you have a chance to convey the desired information all the more successfully.

Giving Choice Is So Important

Having a decision of how and when to see or hear your organization's message fits in splendidly with the way that your potential clients live their lives today. It can likewise convey more weight and viability, as you are not smashing your organization's message down the throat of each poor, clueless individual that strolls by.

This is one reason why podcasts are as well known as they may be. We as a whole have sucha brief period on our hands nowadays, and we are besieged with truly heaps of advertising messages every single day. However, with a podcast, it very well may be downloaded and tuned in to at home, busy working, on the train, on the cylinder, in actuality anyplace.

Utilizing Podcasts For Expert Status

One massively profitable part of utilizing podcasting as part of your showcasing procedure is the thing that it can accomplish for your situating.

So, what precisely do I mean by that?

Delivering a podcast can permit your business to make an essential way of life as an innovator in your field while improving your believability as well. By doing this, you could rapidly end up turning into an expert in your industry, which is no awful thing.

It is likewise incredibly farfetched that any of your rivals will do podcasting, or some other critical promoting procedures so far as that is concerned thus straight away you're more than a stride in front of them.

You Can use This Guerrilla Marketing Strategy

Why not, as a method for including more an incentive for your audience members, talk with a portion of your top clients, and utilize these meetings as amazing promoting instruments for your business?

By doing this, what you are doing is utilizing something many refer to as 'social evidence.' Social evidence is actually what a tribute is, and by having this in audio position, this will be limitlessly more impressive than a composed tribute.

This will help possibilities to envision precisely why they ought to work with you, rather than your closest rivals.

It likewise concretes your clout in your given industry.

It would likewise be shrewd to utilize these same chronicles as tributes and have them put on your site, so guarantee that you ask the clients that you're talking to voice their assessment of your items or administrations.

Also, you could make client dedication as a large portion of us like to be asked our suppositions on something, and this may show to your top clients that they are to be sure esteemed and that their perspectives and conclusions do check.

The Double Whammy Effect Takes Place

This might have a one-two punch impact on your business too. In any case, you could get some fantastic exposure from doing this as your clients will cherish you for it, in addition to you're ready to exhibit your ability in your particular territory of business.

The one-two punch impact happens because this will thus upgrade your validity, and how you are seen by your friends, rivals, forthcoming clients, and your present customers.

Your contenders will likewise be both challenging and stressed regarding what you are doing.

Why Not Use Your Competition To Your Advantage?

So, all things considered, why not meet your rivals? For whatever length of time that you position it accurately, they will presumably gladly have you talk with them as it will give them so reputation and exposure, anyway as it is you talking with them, you will be seen as the master, and not them.

So, they're getting what they need, which is some exposure, but on the other hand, you're getting what you need, which is improved validity of your master status.

Furthermore, in case you're in any way like me, you'll presumably know from your own experience that a great many people love to talk about their mastery, their family, and only by and large about themselves.

This implies you most likely know a few people that chatter endlessly about what they've done for the current week, a week ago and a month ago. These could be a prime possibility for the meeting, and as you will be viewed as the master, the advantages to your business could be gigantic.

The Trouble With Podcasting

I can't help thinking that numerous little to medium estimated organizations like having their digital broadcast and have heard that they are useful for business. Accordingly, we get a lot of inquiries about the account and webcast creation. Be that as it may, a ton of work and time is engaged with delivering a customary webcast and can end up being very overwhelming for the new podcaster. It is consequently nothing unexpected that a decent number of inquiries don't transform into web recordings.

I feel that there are some legitimate explanations behind this.

Cost

The expense of expertly delivered web recordings can be restrictive for little to medium estimated organizations who are new to the universe of podcasting. As far as we can tell, digital broadcast is just compelling as an arrangement, with the account and creation costing somewhere in the range of 150 GBP to 500 GBP for each webcast, contingent upon the intricacy and association of expert voiceovers and sound altering administrations.

With a reasonable expense of around 300 GBP for web recording creation and a progression of at any rate six shows, the money related speculation is critical; in any case, if you get the substance of the digital broadcast arrangement right, you ought to get a stable profit for your venture. Increasingly about this later.

Commonplace expenses can include: -

Utilizing proficient voiceovers

Area recording

Blending, altering, and creation

Incorporation of audio cues and music

Whenever done appropriately, the advantages of your web recording arrangement will far exceed the expenses for a long time. Once on the web, it very well may be gotten to and delighted in by a large number of individuals around the globe. Try to pitch the digital broadcast content accurately to your objective market. On the off chance that you are business disapproved and approach your web recording starting here of view, it might bode well to attempt to cover your speculation by selling Podverts (digital recording adverts) to potential supporters. This works just by putting one or various poverty inside the substance of your digital broadcast appear. The advantages of this are evident as the support will have their product(s) publicized to the entirety of your audience members. Besides, your audience members will be in a specific market gathering, and it bodes well for correlative industry areas to jump aboard with your digital broadcast arrangement from the earliest starting point. At first, this will most likely be progressively troublesome as you don't have a demonstrated reputation; however, once you have a fruitful arrangement added to your repertoire, you ought to have audience calculates that you can intrigue supports with.

Your supporters can take care of one expense for their podvert, or you could offer a rebate for buying numerous podvert spaces. In a 10 to 15 moment digital broadcast, I don't think it impossible to have 3-4 short adverts/support messages splitting subject portions. Given your sound makers are cautious about the situation and number of podverts, your audience members will acknowledge these as a significant aspect of the bundle; we are used to seeing and hearing adverts.

Once your web recording is built up, you can take this idea a phase further by offering an ad highlight to your support, for instance, a meeting about their item as well as administrations. For whatever length of time that the component is applicable and offers an incentive to your objective market, this also will be acknowledged as a feature of the bundle. This, as of now, occurs on radio shows and TV. More often than not, we don't understand we are being publicized.

Digital recording content

This is likely the primary motivation that a web recording never develops into an arrangement and is presumably the hardest part for most organizations to get their heads around. Composing the content for a web recording can be tedious and very hard, to begin with; notwithstanding, when you have a vibe for it, such as everything else throughout everyday life, it gets simpler. On the off chance that you genuinely battle with this, there is no motivation behind why you can't utilize the administrations of a scriptwriter and give yourself the situation of the inventive executive. By and by, I accept that it is increasingly imperative to locate a topic that is fascinating and significant to your objective market than making an ideal content. Conceptualizing with partners and even customers about potential points, subjects, highlights, meetings, and amusement things will before long give you a harsh blueprint of substance that can be the crude material for your content.

When you have the layout for your first digital broadcast and potentially your second, the state of the arrangement will become more transparent, and from this, you ought to have the option to make a show format. It is a smart thought to test these underlying thoughts with a couple of individuals before heading off to the cost of having an expert web recording recorded and delivered. When you are content with the general views of your digital broadcast appear, you should either content it for an expert Voice-over to describe (typically progressively great) or host the webcast yourself.

The decision to utilize an expert voiceover or doing the portrayal yourself is one that you have to take. There are acceptable and terrible focuses onboth of these. If you are not used to talking to a receiver, the outcomes could be truly awful for the audience, and therefore, numerous individuals may turn off and never listen again. Then again, are acceptable at talking into a receiver and can extend the perfect measure of a character, you may turn into a hit with your crowd. The away form of utilizing an expert voiceover is that your web recording will sound cleaned and increasingly like a radio show. In any case, you have to conclude which would be additionally speaking to your audience members/target advertise.

If you conclude that turning into the host is a tad of a stretch for you, some organizations can compose the administrations of an expert voiceover for you.

There are different ways that a decent maker can fuse components of area recording with a studio-created voiceover to give a shifted and real complexity in the web recording creation. For example, it is simple for a voiceover to present a 5-minute meeting or a 5-minute visit you had in the workplace with an associate or business contact. The complexity between the two will make a variety for the audience. For instance, I have known digital broadcast meetings to be completed on trains, planes, bars, dance clubs, and even limos.

Try not to be hesitant to be inventive. Being diverse can assist you with standing apart from your rivals and could be the factor that gets you acknowledgment by your objective market and industry.

We are getting it out there!

Digital broadcast advertising is a significant subject, and as an organization, the ideal approach to get your webcast to the correct audience members is to let them know legitimately. Utilize your customer list/mailing list, all things considered, these are individuals that have an enthusiasm for your item and administrations since they have either utilized your administrations or joined your mailing list. If you have a bulletin that you send to customers on your mailing show, you could make a sound rendition of it or advance your new digital recording arrangement on your pamphlet.

Alright, so you have a mailing rundown of 20,000 individuals that you have sent your most recent bulletin to; you tell everyone that you have an incredible new digital broadcast and everybody tunes in to it not precisely. Even though the vast majority have known about the term digital recording and think they comprehend what it is, there are still loads of individuals that don't have the foggiest idea what podcasting is, the place to discover webcasts or how to hear them out.

When promoting your digital broadcast, direct your mailing list supporters of a page on your site or blog that unmistakably clarifies and instructs them about your webcast, the listening choices accessible, and how to buy into future web recording appears.

Many individuals don't understand that a digital recording can be effortlessly tuned in to from their PC, iPod or mp3 player, or copied to CD for tuning in at home or in the vehicle. Numerous individuals don't understand that their time, mainly during drives, can be utilized as significant digital broadcast listening time. You could be the one to teach and engage them using your web recording; they will be ever thankful to you for this.

Contingent upon your spending limit and item, an extraordinary business advancement is offered your top customers a reciprocal blessing, an mp3 player, for instance, pre-stacked with your digital recordings and even organization marked. Some organizations produce a marked product, for example, pens, mugs, napkins, and so forth, who might do likewise with your special blessing.

When you have your web recording supporters, you have to keep them tuning in. Requesting audience feeling and criticism will help refine your digital recording arrangement to keep them drew in and anxiously anticipating the following show and, potentially, your new method. You could do this just on your site by requesting criticism or having a remarks box on your blog. It is a smart thought to offer a motivation for giving criticism, for example, a prize attracts to win another iPod, blessing vouchers, and so forth.

I enthusiastically suggest that you have your digital broadcast interpreted and accessible as content on your site or blog. The explanation behind this is that web crawlers can't break down the substance of your sound, and they can dissect and list literary content. Your transcript will contain the entirety of your pertinent watchwords and key expressions that will draw in the web search tools and pull in new audience members and potential new customers. This is a perfect spot to have your remark box.

Observing

When your first digital broadcast arrangement is out there, you have to screen its viability. Time and cash have been put into the account and creation of your digital recording, so you have to see an advantageous profit for your speculation. This can estimated in different manners, in any case, the critical goals of your webcast ought to be to:-

Concrete existing connections among you and your customers and furnish them with included worth.

Draw in new customers using your web recording on the web and using referrals from existing audience members.

Increment mindfulness about your items and administrations and to spread your message.

Stay with you in front of your rivals.

If you can accomplish the entirety of this while getting supporters to take care of the expense of your web recording production.

Kind reader,

Thank you very much. I hope you enjoyed the book.

Can I ask you a big favor?

I would be grateful if you would please take a few minutes to leave me a gold star on Amazon.

Thank you again for your support.

Simon Edwards

www.ingramcontent.com/pod-product-compliance
Lightning Source LLC
Chambersburg PA
CBHW080500220526
45465CB00006B/2324